finding
daisies

jessica jocelyn

Finding Daisies

ISBN 9798805427146

Illustrations: Janelle Parraz
Cover design: Janelle Parraz and Jessica Jocelyn
Fonts by saltandpepperfonts

for my sister,
who left nursing
during quarantine
to protect the life
of my unborn child

and for Rachel,
who pretends not to mind when I tell her all
these stories over and over

there is no clear timeline to this story, to protect certain identities

to heal a wildflower,
y o u m u s t f i r s t g o t o h e r r o o t s.
to get to her roots
you have to go back to the beginning.
l e t's g o b a c k t o t h e b e g i n n i n g.

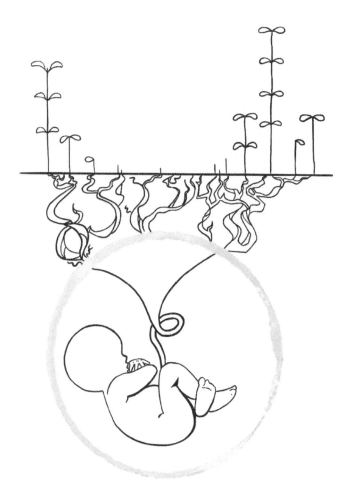

THE ROOTS.

jessica jocelyn

I was wanted.
with every bit of her being,
the collection of cells
growing inside her
rearranging every time
he raised his voice to her,
reshuffling each time she fired back.

I wove her fire
and his lies
into my being,
and there I was,
designed with a heart already broken.

I wonder sometimes who I could've been
had he loved her right
had he loved us right.

instead, here I am
made from the fire within her
and the lies inside him.

a moment in time,
that happened so long ago.
one of the first memories I still recall,
it's so dark
and I'm being carried by a man.
he brought me inside an apartment
that I don't recognize.
later I learned
that it was our new home.
my mother, my sister, and I,
we left in the middle of the night
because we had to.
afterwards my mother
gripped me so tight
crying.
I feel with all my heart
that she died in my arms that night
and she never got the healing
she required.
without healing, she'd never be capable
of being the mother we needed.
when a man walks away from his family,
he destroys so much more
than anyone can ever begin to comprehend.
the consequences of his actions
spanned decades.

and that's how my father
took my mother from me.

he was the first man
to say he was glad I was his,
and the first man to deny
my existence.

he was the first man
to say he'd stay for always,
and the first man
to walk out the door.

he was the first man
to proclaim undying love for me,
and the first man
to prove he didn't mean it.

he wouldn't be the last man
to do all these things,
but there's just a certain wound
that forms
when that man is the one who created you.

he didn't just leave *you,*
he didn't just leave *her and I,*
he left *all of us.*
he left to make a new family,
a new life
a do over, as he would say.

you, her, and me,
we are from the same story
but I think it drove us further apart.
perhaps the color of our eyes
were just reminders too painful
of how you thought your life would be.

her hair is long
and dark.
her skin, very fair.
she is excited for today.
her father is coming to pick her up
to spend time with her.
she takes time to pick out a dress
perhaps, maybe the color would please him.
bows tied to the ends of her hair,
she waits on the front porch-
time passes
minutes like hours, hours like eternity.
her mother wants her to come inside
but, surely, he is coming, right?
don't want to miss him.
more time passes
minutes like hours, hours like eternity.
she starts to count the tiny red hearts
on her white tights.
37, there are 37.
the sky is dark now.
he never ends up coming
and not the day after that, either.
her physical body went back into the house
but not her whole heart-
in a way
she will always be that little girl
waiting on the porch
for someone who will never come.

the date was August 15, 1992. I was in the backyard with all my cousins. everyone ate pizza and the adults drank Coors beer. they said it made sense since my grandfather had worked for Coors and it was his favorite beer. there were lots of pizzas but I couldn't find one without olives. I remember how they tasted. bitter.

I knew my grandpa was very sick with cancer. glioblastoma, but I didn't know what that meant. my mom told me that they tried to operate but couldn't get it all. that sounded so stupid to me. why wouldn't they get it all? we would go to visit him sometimes at the nursing home. I never knew what to say to him, but I remember he never liked us to see him take out his teeth as he was getting ready for bed. so, my sister and I would always turn around.

my mom came back to the party with her sisters and my grandmother. she walked up to me and told me that he had died. she said they read Psalm 23 to him and read the Footprints in the Sand poem. I didn't know what that was, so she explained it to me. The story was about a man looking back at his life and seeing two pairs of footprints in the sand. he noticed during the hardest parts of his life there was only one pair. and it was because that was when God was carrying him. I wondered if I was being carried at that moment. or if I had been in the past. and I decided that I felt alone simply because I was alone. and my grandfather wasn't looking down at us from heaven because how could he possibly be watching the family he built be torn apart while still being amongst paradise?

I haven't touched an olive since that day. and the family that he had built, was never the same.

is heaven a destination
or a place that is easily touched?
mine was a moment in time
that occurred only during springtime
in the central valleys of California.
150 acres of almond blossoms
and as the petals fell,
they covered the ground
like snow.
running through them,
I was wild and free.

her skin was the color of
the earth after the rain.
hair piled on top of her head,
her stature short,
though she stood taller than mountains to me.
she was beautiful and warm
and said *I love you*
in two different languages.

as a child,
I always thought it meant she loved me
twice as much
as someone who could only say *I love you*
in one.

abuelita

the women on the tv
are tall, thin, blonde, bronze;
the way he admires them,
set the standard of beauty.
the way his eyes glistened,
told me there could be no exceptions
to this rule.
these were the days of silicone breasts
the increased size
equated their worth.

the girl in the mirror
is short, pale, dark hair
with budding breasts that indicate
the growth to come
might not amount to much.

how will I find my worth now?
being a teenage girl is hard.

it was the way he made me laugh. it was always about the way he made me laugh. the very first sentence he spoke ended with me having the biggest smile in a long time. his voice had such power. he was the first boy to tell me I was beautiful. now I realize he was the first *person* to tell me I was beautiful. one day, we sat for hours after school and sang Disney duets and shared pixy stix. just two extremely sad, lonely kids who wanted nothing more than to know what it felt like to fit somewhere.

how could we not suck each other in?

I was easy to control,
I sought nothing more
than to please everyone,
please him.
I was told how to dress,
how much makeup to wear,
who to talk to
or who not to.

it's because I love you so much

and who was I to disagree
I knew nothing different.

if you love me, then you will

okay, I think I love you.
I never said no,
but my body never said yes.
sometimes I'd rush home
and stand in scalding water
scratching at my flesh.
if this is how it always is,
I wish to hide my body forever.

I was told it never happened,
or I must be remembering wrong.
and although I was seeing things
with my own eyes,
I was taught not to trust them.

scars lined his arms
and I'd ask why he would do that to himself?

I would rather feel this
than what I feel inside.

when he was finally gone
from my life,
I felt so completely confused in my skin
that I searched for anything familiar
to keep my feet on the ground.

I would rather feel this
than what I feel inside.

my scars now match his,
tying me to his ghost
so that even in the death of us,
I still can't escape him.

the doctors and therapists
tell me it's just a phase
that it can be normal to be
so sad all the time.

here, take this,
come back in two weeks.

I'm still so sad
what else can I do?
I just want to feel okay.

here, take more,
come back in two weeks.

I don't know how to explain this
I don't want to die,
but I just can't bear to exist right now.

here, let's add another pill for you to take
this is just a phase
and this will help you get over the slump.

just a phase?
it's not just a phase
if I can feel my will to stay
slowly erode
with each passing day.
but maybe if I'm zombified,
I won't care
if my outcome goes either way.

finding daisies

we bonded through a pain so similar.
our parents refused to be there
as the two black sheep exchanged vows,
but it didn't matter-
the few people who loved us most
were there
and with our tiny paychecks,
we then got on a plane
and flew 2,000 miles away

we never looked back.

our love wasn't about grand gestures
or diamonds,
it was about
climbing to the top of your father's roof
to talk under the stars,
to hop in our tiny blue car
at one in the morning,
to search for deer on back roads
and eating off paper plates
when we couldn't afford anything else.
it was about having nothing,
yet having it all.

jessica jocelyn

don't kiss me in the rain.
kiss me in the middle of a snowfall
as if we are two wolves
that weren't meant for the humid
passion of monsoons,
but the cold bitter winds of winter.

I don't want to get lost in small talk,
let's lie in bed
and listen to me tell you why wind chimes
remind me of my grandmother
and bring me comfort,
and then we can fall asleep to you
telling me how you got the scar on your hip.

let's take a walk in the woods
while you tell me how you believe we turn
into mushrooms when we die
and then we can contemplate our immortality.

let's go grocery shopping
and I'll explain why cutting up kiwis
makes me incredibly sad
and I'll listen to you tell me
about those thick, pillowy sugar cookies
and how they remind you of your sister.

I don't want to know your favorite fruit
but I might tell you mine are strawberries;
what I want to know
is what album you put on repeat
when you felt all alone in the world.

you led me to a mirror.
do you love her?
I stared straight into the girl
looking back at me.
I looked down and whispered
I'm not sure.
you put your hand
gently on my shoulder and explained
then you cannot possibly
love me,
until you love her.

one morning,
the sun grew too tired
and decided her time was done.
her explosion filled the sky
with thick ash
and darkness.
I decided to take her place
and illuminate your world.
I fear one day
the responsibility will become too great
and my time to turn to dust
will come sooner than promised.
until then,
I
am
here.

it's like the moon
waiting all night
for the sun,
only to see it
for brief fleeting moments
as they scrape by each other,
but night after night,
the moon waits anyway.

let me love the darkest parts of you.
show me your scars
so, I may kiss those twice.
bring me to your walls,
the ones you hide behind.
we'll chisel cracks in them
to let the light in.
we'll dance and plant seeds
and grow new memories.

you're like my favorite book to read.
the one I keep returning to
with the cracked spine
and pages bookmarked
with all my favorite spots to visit.
words blurred from random tears
and rips, where I couldn't
turn the pages
fast enough.
the one that I read over and over
even though the ending stays the same.

my hands will reach for you-
every
time.

meet me in the woods
where the old oak fell,
resting high above the mycelium
that holds the knowledge of the forest.

meet me where we can listen
to their songs
lyrics intertwining like our hands.

meet me where they can teach us
that there can be growth
even after death.

finding daisies

oh, what a world
with no social media
no timelines
when it was just you and I
f a c e   t o   f a c e .
no filters.
if I could jump to any time period,
it would be this one.

dreams are a sweet escape
when I know
you are waiting there
on the other side.

his fingers trailed my body.
light touches
here and there-
there were so many
like my body was made of stars
and he paused to count them
and name each one.
this wasn't a race to the finish line
because there was no clear destination.
instead, there were many detours
to make sure it never ended.

slow

if the time ever comes
when you lose yourself,
I will never
stop looking for you.
I will be the one in the dark,
holding a torch,
to help guide you home.

I want the tattoos on my body
to inspire paintings-
the kind where the ideas
get so stuck inside your head.
they drive you mad
and the only way to quiet your mind
is to stay up all night,
bleeding onto the canvas,
pouring both our souls
in a mixture of colors,
never satisfied
because it's just never quite right.

when going through hard times,
in very young adulthood
through tears, I asked my grandmother
what if I can never forgive him?
I'm supposed to forgive.

she took me in her arms
and with all the certainty
in her body told me
we are imperfect humans,
sometimes we just may never forgive
but what we can't forgive
Jesus will cover.

I looked at her
and thought about all the times I felt
I should've been protected
and kept from many bad situations
way beyond my years and control.

Jesus forgives you, mija
she softly said as she stroked my head.

I blinked
I forgive Him, as well.

jessica jocelyn

'

THE AWAKENING.

jessica jocelyn

I feel I may have reached
a point where I became
the very monster
I spent my life
trying to destroy.
they were never hiding under my bed
but rather came in the form
of a beautiful face
or a soft loving hand.
I feel I may have reached
a point where I didn't have time
to decipher between
who was good and who wasn't
so, I struck first
and I struck hard enough
that they'd never bother to get back up.

by now she sees the way
men look at her when she passes by.
her body has become a weapon
but it's her voice
that becomes the unknowing accomplice.
she can weave words,
creating fantasies beyond your capacity
of understanding.
c o m e   h e r e
she whispers
as she takes you to the side
and you follow eagerly,
anticipating her next move,
her next word,
her next touch,
and you'll follow her
even as she leads you to a cliff.
without hesitation,
you will jump,
your last emotion will be regret
as you realize she is not behind you
as promised.

all those years ago,
I was the train wreck
that barreled through
as I stopped at your station.
I couldn't imagine not stopping
to get lost in life with you,
to be young and reckless.
I wanted to love you
with all the broken pieces of my soul.
I didn't know how to tell you to stop,
that I was not good for you.
I was too young to know
that just because I wanted to,
doesn't mean it was something
I was any good at.

I am made of all kinds of good intentions
that just never turned out quite right-
I'm not sure what anyone expected.
I am just the long dark-haired daughter
of an extremely sinful man,
built on lies so magnificent
that even he believed them.
it only made sense that since they flowed
through my veins,
it would come second nature to me.

I am subjective,
just like poetry.
to one, I was an intense love story
but to another, I was the catalyst to
their own personal implosion.

anxiety and depression
are my hidden gifts.
they are the parts I keep for myself.
the ones I give to others
are the giant smiles and laughter.

when you hurt under the surface,
no one can see it or help you.
so, it continues to grow like cancer
in a way that
by the time it does come about,
it's now too late.

I find that you get louder
when you don't really
have anything to say.
your volume is your compensation
for your inability to communicate.

I'm watching as you crumble,
falling to the ground in pieces.
one by one I pick them up
and try to put them back together.

but they don't make glue
for these type of things.

so, I continue
to just swim in your demise.

falling in love with the potential
was my favorite part
the way your fingers
left warmth on my skin,
the way the words
would get caught in my hair
and whisper in my ear
dear potential,
stay just a while longer
for reality is not my friend.

the thing is,
as a child, I always wanted to play fair
and the rules became my favorite part.

but this is love
there are no rules
and no one ever plays fair.

we throw words like daggers,
you and I,
a fight to the death
but out of all the destruction
that flew from our mouths,
it's all the things we never said
that I most regret.

I'm finding it hard to breathe
when your heart is so cold
that you've frozen the air around me.
I've come to realize
that it's just not possible to survive
when you are near.

your hands bruised my skin
and
your words bruised my heart,
but what's worse
is your soul
swallowed mine whole.

oh, the sticks and the stones.

I'm not sober
but it's not what you think.
I've fallen off the wagon
as I've picked up the phone,
and dialed your number.
I swear I could do it in my sleep
as sometimes I do.
I know I shouldn't
but I want to feel something.
I'm addicted to the highs and lows
and most of the time I don't know
what to do.

they don't have rehabs
for situations like these.

I saw the texts with my own eyes
and still you told me
that it didn't happen.
your word was enough for my brain
to tell my heart that you
were telling the truth
because no one can gaslight me
better than myself.

I frantically grabbed his shirt
filling both fists with fabric.

was it hard to love me?

my eyes looked into his,
pleading for answers.

was it easy to turn to her?

I didn't need a response,
especially when any answer
was always the wrong one.
of course, it was easy
since with me, it required work
and anything worth a damn
isn't just given to you.

if you're going to stab me
in the back,
turn me around first,
look me in the eye.
stab me in the front
instead.

it's the least you could do.

this letter is the final step in closing this chapter in my life. I don't even know you, but you've impacted my life in so many ways. I chose to take the selfish decisions you made and turn them into positives in moving forward with my life.

I used to think that it was unfair that I was in so much pain while you probably were sleeping well at night. and then someone helped me see that that couldn't possibly be true. you see, I am growing stronger every day, into a version that is better than before. and you, well you will have to live with the guilt and embarrassment of your actions. actions that have revealed voids in your heart and in your soul. holes that lead to even deeper issues. only a mentally weak woman will continue to pursue a man after she discovers he is married and be content to be kept in the shadows and thrown scraps. you should want more for yourself.

I used to wonder who you were, but discovered your actions told me exactly all I needed to know. somewhere along the line, you felt disappointed and unseen by someone important in your life. you seek to fill that void with the approval of any person you meet, it doesn't matter who. I urge you to find out where that comes from and learn to heal from it. every decision we make in this world affects others, which is why we must think carefully before we act. and trust me, the next wife will not be as nice as I was. I release all the negativity you brought into my life and am giving it back to you. you've already taken enough of my time and energy and not one more second will be spent on you.

the letter I gave to the other woman

give me back my sleep.
you owe me so much sleep.
the deep kind
where not even a thunderstorm
enters my dreams.
the kind so peaceful,
the dead would be jealous.

give me back my time.
you owe me so much time.
the kind well spent,
even the kind where nothing special happens.

you owe me so much.

I understood women more that day
more specifically
my mother,
my grandmother,
my mother-in-law.
my view of the world changed
almost like when Dorothy saw Oz in color
but in reverse.
to go through life and do as you're told
grow an entire human being
and not just their organs
but setting the groundwork
for their hopes and dreams
body pushed to the limit
you grow,
you stretch,
you rip,
you tear,
you age
and, with every wrinkle
society deducts your worth
and just when you feel
you have your head above water,
you are traded in
by someone who you discovered
probably never realized your value.

I understood women more that day
more specifically the ones who I always
called bitter
with a sour taste in my mouth.
you then cross into the side

where you can identify this kind of pain
and not just by the way it feels
but by the way it leads you.

I understood women more that day
more specifically the ones
who spoke of their broken hearts
until the day they finally fell asleep in death.

I understood women more that day
more specifically the ones
who tucked the pain deep inside
for another day
because they knew small eyes were watching.

I understood women more that day
more specifically the ones
who didn't just give up
either on themselves,
but mostly on their children
the ones who didn't make the easy decisions
but the right ones.

I understood women more that day
more specifically their strength
so I put on another coat of mascara
laced my shoes
and knew I had to keep moving
and carry on their legacy.

finding daisies

men rarely upgrade when they cheat.
it was a joke I heard in whispers
as a child.
I didn't understand it fully
even when I saw the woman
my father left us for
and started a new life with.
I didn't find her face very appealing
but it was really her heart
that made her ugly.
the words that spilled from her mouth
like toxic waste.
she'd scream at me that she did things
better than my mother did
until cops came and told us visitation
was just not going to happen *again.*
I would get poked
by my mother's broken heart
and with tears in my eyes wondered,
this is what you left us for?
life has a way of coming back for you
as last I heard she was riddled with sores
from putting too much poison inside her.
men rarely upgrade when they cheat.
they find women just as broken and weak.
someone convenient
someone that requires no effort.
and if this made you feel better
reading this,
know that she doesn't hold a candle to you
and if this made you feel
some sort of animosity,

then I urge you to look inside yourself
and figure out why.

beware of the woman
who is upfront with trying
to pass as a unicorn
flaunting her facade to all
and dripping with nauseating sweetness.
a real unicorn hides her magic
from the world
because she knows there are many
in search of her to steal her horn.
she only reveals herself to a few lucky ones
and makes you work
to view her magic.

jessica jocelyn

there is a certain type of pain so raw
when you scream towards the heavens,
begging for the secret code there must be
to learn how to un-love someone.

when I wake up in the morning, it feels as
though my chest is cut wide open and there is
nothing inside the cavity. I sit up and must
search around the room to find my heart. once I
find her, I give her a tiny kiss and whisper how
sorry I am that she's hurting so badly. I place
her back into my chest and sew it back up,
feeling every stitch from a rusty needle, every
pull of the thread. tears fall down my cheeks
from the sting of it all. I go through my day
and curse the sun for still shining while it is so
dark inside myself. every step I take feels like
shards of glass have been hidden in the grass.

this is what a broken heart feels like to me.

I stopped talking to you
because you stopped listening to
what I had to say-
I'm sure that you heard every word
every single time
but when I stopped talking
and started listening with my eyes,
they told me all I needed to know.

you can't wear me down for years
with your words
breaking all my bones
and expect me to still have the same shape.
my body has healed since then
but the form I took on is different.
these hands don't look the same
and they no longer want to reach for you.
my face has gotten older
and it no longer yearns to turn towards yours.

he watched me beg
and listened to me plead
to get him to try
and finally, stop and change.
by the time he did,
I wasn't the same woman
who was doing all that pleading
and the change wasn't even
wanted anymore.

I sat in my pain with you for so long
that I needed that final moment
to rock my world so hard
that I finally lost my footing.

it shook me awake
you clung to me so tight
that when I pushed you away,
you ripped the version of me that loved you.
ripped it straight from my bones.

underneath is a version so new and scared
and I am meeting her for the first time.

you aren't allowed to love her.

the day we signed our divorce papers,
I walked in front of you to leave.
I stopped at the door and turned to you.
we both cried.
we apologized for not loving each other well
but how could we?
we didn't know how
we were still children.
unfortunately, we used each other
to learn that some things just can't be undone.
I touched your face
and became overwhelmed with sadness
since I knew one day I'd forget exactly
what shade of blue your eyes were,
or the way your face felt under my hand.
we knew we'd never see each other again
after this.
how silly now we were shedding tears
showing emotions that we bottled.
shared apologies
when it no longer mattered.
how surreal to know we were about to become
strangers again.
mourning the death of each other
even though we knew the other
was still in existence.
our last moments together were full of
understanding and kindness.
imagine if we applied that during
the whole marriage?
we probably could've made it.

sometimes, I think I need to
have just one more conversation
with you,
tell you everything
I think I need to say,
but it doesn't take long
for me to remember
that you've heard it all before
and I am now here
while you are still there
and it will change nothing.
so, I stay silent.

when writing the story of us,
will they speak of magic
or will they describe the holes
we left that the other can't fill?
all the different ways we tried
to make things fit
but were left with all the echoes
of broken dreams
bouncing off the hollow walls
of our hearts.

my toxic trait is
being convinced that
even from thousands
of miles away
and years apart,
I believe
that you still love me.

there is a place between night and morning
the small phase of peace
between sleeping and waking.
the tiny interval between
needing and wanting.
that space
that is where I always seem to find you-
find us
there is where I will always love you.

I don't know how to let you go.
there are parts of me that I gave you
that I've never gotten back.
I suppose I never asked for them though;
I hope that you kept them.

I heard our old maple tree fell,
the one we used to climb
when we were young.
I went to find her and there she was,
she had grown very old
and had just felt the weight of the world
for too long.
she was home to many things
but once she was done, they left.
I reached out to touch her
to see if I could still feel her spirit
and with tears in my eyes,
I decided that I no longer could.
I whispered to her that I understood
and knew she had to leave
oh, how alike we had become.

when I was a child, I took colored chalk and draw landscapes on the cracked driveway. they never turned out as good as my sister's, but that never bothered me. back then, a California rainstorm wasn't so few and far between and they blew in to try and wash all my hard work away. I sat in the living room and pushed my nose to the huge plate glass just watching it. the colors blurred and mixed. there was nothing I could do as I helplessly watched it all become unrecognizable and finally bleed away.

that was a lot like falling in and out of love with you. I tried so hard to create something so beautiful. and even though I felt someone else could do it better, I still wanted to be the one to create the art with you. and just like the weather I couldn't control, the circumstances just happened and there was a point where all I could do was just watch it all wash away.

and nothing left to do but let it.

how do you forget someone
whose unique fingerprint
you still find on your skin?
how do you close your eyes
and not see their face anymore?

they tell me to be grateful for the pain, that it has shown me how strong I can be. they speak of resilience. maybe I already knew that strength inside. maybe I didn't need something so painful to show me. maybe I'd rather be the girl I was before. the one who believed in magic and happy ever afters. maybe I'd rather have that innocence back, be that small naive girl once more. maybe I'd rather base my worth off how much beauty surrounds me and not how many times I crawled back up. maybe I'd rather know the girl I could've been.

sometimes
    all
      I
        think
          about
            is

                    her

I truly think
that forgiveness means different things
to different people.
forgiving means letting go of the pain,
but I'm terrified that if I let go,
I will forget
and I don't want to forget.
I need to always remember how it felt
so, it can guide me.

jessica jocelyn

I wonder if
it's harder there on the other side
without someone to offer
as your sacrifice
now that you're falling
without
a
parachute
and
no
cushion
to
break
your
fall

(me)

sweet child,
you are changing seasons.
I must rip you from this earth
and place you where you truly belong.
yes, it will hurt.
yes, you will be scared.
no, it will not be easy
but first, your heart must break
to the point where leaving
is the only chance for survival.
awaken, child.
awaken by the pain.
come back to life.

jessica jocelyn

THE HEALING.

jessica jocelyn

who I was before you were born
became irrelevant
with each surge of pain.
we moved
in a dance
only you and I could understand.

I could feel myself dying
as I transcended realms
filled with sacred geometry
forming tessellations
of moments in time
showing me
a small girl, alone and
a teenage girl, scared and bleeding.   `

as I traveled back to the present,
we urged both of them to come with us.
you shot out into existence,
my screams stopped
and yours began,
picking up where I left off.

we sucked in deep
breathing our first breaths
as we are both
born.
you, for the first time
and me, once more.

I wasn't sure if I would have children
until one day, there he was.
the first time he called me mama
was the first time I had ever felt safe.
I spent my life trying to squeeze into places
where I wasn't quite sure I fit
let alone belonged.
and here he was,
my fleshly earth-side home.

jessica jocelyn

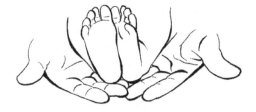

the moment we met,
your eyes locked on mine
and suddenly, everything made sense.

all the mistakes
that ended on broken dirt roads
every tear
every scar
every decision that ended in disaster
led me here
led me to you.

and who knew that taking
a wrong turn with you
ended up being right all along?

how could I possibly begin
to poeticize motherhood?
how could I ever explain fully to someone
that it has brought me to my weakest
moments
yet made me a stronger version than before?
how I lost my voice
but gained another big enough
to speak loud enough for all of us?
that I'm sad I'm not who I was
or have what I had before
but gained things so incredible
that it's impossible to imagine my life
without them.

you're having trouble sleeping tonight
and back and forth to your crib, I've been.
as I'm rocking you, I realize
that all you want in the world is me
and at this moment,
I'm teaching you
that I will always be there when you cry.
you can always lay the weight of your world
down on my chest.
I close my eyes and breathe you in deep.
you won't always smell this way.
you won't always call for me
in the middle of the night.
there will come a time when
you won't even be sleeping in my house
any longer.
once these moments are gone,
they're gone forever
and no amount of bargaining
will bring them back.
so, for now
it's 5 more minutes of rocking
one more lullaby
to cement in your mind,
I will always be here.

we walked into the room and sat down.

"we're here to talk about your son's results from the testing we did last month."

I gripped my husband's hand tightly and took a deep breath.

"we found that your son does test within the autism spectrum. in the high functioning range."

her mouth kept moving, but I heard no words. I left that room and was immediately back in the tiny delivery room feeling the weight of his body on my chest 7 years prior. all 8 pounds, 6 ounces of him, yet he felt like so much more. he had so much long black hair, which explained the excruciating heartburn I had felt my whole pregnancy. he didn't cry much, almost as if he felt it would just waste his time. his eyes were so wide and alert as he looked up at me.

I came back to the room to start focusing on her words and why they felt he placed in the spectrum. the diagnosis was not a surprise to me; it was something I had always known deep inside me. but it was still very painful to hear. life is so hard. extremely hard. and now he was going to have to navigate all those difficult roads with added hardship. I began to mourn his future. it was silent but manifested into a panic attack that I swallowed.

her voice broke through my thoughts once more.

". social cues will be difficult for him. Empathy could also be something hard for him to grasp."

empathy.

how will I ever teach him empathy?
wasn't that something that was just given to us at birth? programmed into our souls?

it was my main concern as he grew older.

years later, I sat with him in our living room, having the hardest conversation I ever had with him. I was explaining to him as gently as I could that his daddy was very sick, and for our safety, we needed to leave.

he looked up at me, his green eyes full of understanding as he nodded.

"I know he's sick, mama."

my eyes stung, but I refused to cry in front of him. he reached out and touched my hand.

he had come a long way. at one time, he wouldn't let me hold his hand.

"we will be okay. you have me. you always have me."

all his life, I doubted if I was doing a good enough job. if I was who he needed or if I was enough. and in that moment, I knew.

I was doing a good job.
I was who he needed.
I was enough.
and no matter what, we would be okay.

having children is terrifying
but not the way that you'd think.
they come into this world
and there they are,
ready for molding.
but will my boys grow up to be good men?
will my daughter choose a mate wisely?
or if she doesn't, will she have
the strength to leave?
how will they handle
their first real heartbreak?
will it scar them so they never love again?
will they invite the lonely child to
sit with them at lunch?
or will they be the child who sits alone and
wishes every night for a friend?
my heart rips to shreds knowing one day they
will feel the pain of a lie
when they each left my body, I tried to leave
them with a wish.
almost like a fairy godmother would.

to my boys
who I will raise
to only use kind hands
and to my daughter
who I will teach
to accept nothing less

my daughter's hair is getting longer.
I love to keep it clean and brush it.
as I smooth her bangs
away from her eyes,
I stare deep into her.
and with every microdot of my soul
I say,
"you are so beautiful.
I am so lucky
to have you.
I love you."
it is an everyday occurrence
but it's anything but mundane
every time I am brushing her hair
I am also brushing the waist-length black hair
of a 7-year-old me
gently moving her bangs
and wiping the tears from her eyes.
I say to her
"you are so beautiful. they don't say
it, but they are lucky to have you. I
love you."

a mother doesn't just
create you and your wings,
she teaches you how to use them
for so long, I never knew
what to do with them,
so I'm learning now
with the help of my children.
what magnificent little teachers
they've turned out to be.

jessica jocelyn

my smallest loves,
I loved you so hard and so furiously
because I never wanted you to feel alone,
to feel unwanted.
I never wanted you to question
if you were loved
beautiful
smart
talented.
I wanted to fill your cup up so full
that you could easily recognize
when someone was giving you less
and reject it with grace.

I heard you were asking
about me,
about everything I created,
everything I've built
almost as though
they were things you could brag about.
I'm sure it's never crossed your mind
that they aren't yours to claim.
your blood may run through them
but they are nothing like you.
they are warm and kind.
I hope the next time
their names try to leave your mouth,
the universe wraps around you
and sucks the air from your lungs.
no me importa

I've heard of miracles
and prayed for one to come.
I didn't want to learn
to live without her.
the world would be too dark and cold.
the miracle never came.
my words were heard
but that's just not how
it all works.
I now accept it.

I knew she was gone.
she hadn't texted me back in weeks
and I didn't hear the creaking of her rocking
chair as I walked by her door.

I thought I was doing well
being strong.
I was sitting in the pediatrician's office for
my son's yearly physical.
we were updating all his records and
insurance information.

she looked at a paper and said, "now for your
emergency contact, we have Victoria-"

I don't even know if she finished her name.
my breath was stolen and my tongue sank
into my stomach. I let out a noise I didn't
recognize and all the tears came.

the tears I couldn't shed when she died
the tears I couldn't shed at her funeral
there they were

grieving her was a luxury that I couldn't
afford at the time.
sometimes, we are so busy being the rock for
our family that we forget it is okay and
necessary to be soft.

sooner or later, grief catches up with you
and there I was

grieving her in the middle of a doctor's office
with an audience of strangers.
she handed me a tissue and gently said, "we
can do this another time."

"no ma'am, it's clear we need to do this now."

the scariest part of losing you
is my memories of you
f a d i n g   a w a y
almost like grains of sand
slipping through my fingers.
and the more I try to grip on to them,
the faster they seem to go.
maybe if I write them down,
I can hold on to them forever.

things I don't want to forget-
the cackle you made after you told
an awful story,
the way your feet never seemed to stay still,
how I could hear your rocking chair
just before I opened your door,
the time you told me Sandra Bullock
was prettier than me,
the way we laughed afterwards,
when you sewed my teddy bear back together,
the way you kissed my leg after I gave birth
and whispered *thank you* to me.

I'm stuck in between
where I was and where I want to be.
far from better days,
either the ones long ago
or the ones promised ahead.
I'm trying so hard to move on
but it's the forward pace
I just can't seem to get the hang of.

who I thought I was
is such a far cry
from who I really am-
and once I honored her,
I shed the people
who really didn't love me
like a second skin
I never knew I didn't need.

she was so bright
it was as if she bathed in sunflowers,
with bright yellow petals
that lead down to a black center
as she could easily gravitate
towards the darkness.
she was built from the brightest of days
and the loneliest of nights.
her love always came in seasons
intense with the summer
then leaving you cold in the winter
sneaking parts of her
that become embedded
deep inside you
awakening parts of you
that you thought you had forgotten.

my legacy to leave
is not about the times
where people failed me.

it's not about the tear-stained pillows
or the times I was brought to my knees.

when I walk by,
people won't speak
of my dark days.

they will marvel at all the times
I got back up
and kept walking
even though each step
seemed harder than the one before it.

because the ultimate goal is
when my children speak of strength,
they will point to me.

life is not a sequence of straight facts
but a string of experiences.
when things happen to us-
it's hard to make a clean decision
because too many factors come into play.
the people who came
and brought either love or hate,
the lessons they taught you
from the outside looking in
it's easy for others to give advice
based on facts,
but they aren't playing
with the whole deck of cards.
they don't have the experiences
that go with it
so, when someone tells you
oh, I would never.
I would definitely do this instead!"
it's all useless
because they weren't there
and you can't navigate a situation correctly
if you've never been there before.
rather,
put your hand to the mirror
and tell that girl
"it's okay, we've never
been through this before
and we will do better next time."

all my life,
I've been loved (or thought I was)
by people who have always given me
bare minimum
but I'm here to tell you (them)
that you get no praise for being
bare minimum.
not here
not now
and definitely never from me.

I am a mortal woman,
my bones are not meant for you to take to
build your home.
my flesh is not available for you to steal
to keep you warm.
you may take me as your love,
but
I am not your mother.
I am not here to provide you with
what she did not.
I am not here for you to punish her through me
I am not going to stitch up
the unhealed wounds she left,
give it a kiss and send you on your way.
I am not going to teach you how to be
a man or teach you the meaning of consequences.
you need to come to me already whole.
I cannot give you any pieces of me,
there's none to spare.
and finally,
I am not here to prepare you
on how to love the next one the right way.
you aren't allowed to practice on me.

I have found love in its purest form
when it comes straight from
the eyes of a child.

I have found silence,
the peaceful kind
when among the trees
and reaching upward.

I have found desert sunsets
and crystal-clear water
and satisfaction after a long hard day's work.

I believe in all the life I've lived
I've found everything-
everything
but closure.

my path was never easy
and things happened to me
that I never deserved.
I tried to fight hard against them
and never accept it
but the hard truth is that they happened-
they are a part of me
a part of my story
and in between the hardest chapters to read
are beautiful moments
amazing things
and no amount of tragedy
can take that from me.

I love to wear all black
to match the color of the wool
that you say I am
but you see,
you have it all wrong.
nothing about me says sheep.
I've always fought against what was wrong
even if it came from your mouth.
I wasn't made to neatly fit in your box
or follow the paths you found more appealing.

my name is said in whispers
but most of the time not at all.
yet when you do ever utter my name,
do me the one courtesy,
don't refer to me as the black sheep.
I prefer the black wolf,
the one who broke free
with nothing but one suitcase full of clothes
and built myself from the ground up.

oh,
you see,
you have it all wrong
nothing about me says sheep
it screams wolf.

one day,
I will wake up
and have the most amazing day
and won't feel the need
to tell you about it.
that's how I'll know
I'm healing.

I don't recall life before depression
almost like I wasn't created
with all the right pieces.
I'm sure there were plenty missing
that my father had stolen,
so, my mother wasn't able to give them to me.
I'd go through my life seeking
to find those pieces,
thinking maybe they were deep inside
the souls of other people.
I am accepting
that I was designed broken
still functioning.
this is just who I am,
how I was built
fragmented by design
and that's okay.

should we drown in these tears
or run and gather supplies to build a boat?
sink or swim?
we get to decide.

finding daisies

sometimes we don't see the signs
because we didn't know
we were supposed
to be looking for them.

the bad thing about experience
is you have to first get burned
to learn that fire is hot.

you have to sometimes
be touched in all the wrong ways
to discover
how you're supposed to be loved.

and you only can truly grasp
the depth of pain that you've caused
once it has come full circle
back to you.

I won't let what you've done to me
turn my world dark
and leave my heart cold.
if this is going to change me,
then I choose to let it be
for the better.

love yourself first
irrevocably,
unconditionally.
the rest will fall into place.

not everyone is meant for the healing journey
and not all of us arrive
at that same finish line.
some will stay marching in place
to the beat of the very drum that broke them
but never even make it a foot away.
healing is a very messy ride
that requires work that some just will never
have it in them to put forth,
but, here you are
peeling yourself off the floor,
wiping away the smeared makeup
from yesterday,
and strapping on those boots
for the long road ahead.
the ugly, dark road that you have no choice
but to travel through to get to the other side.
be proud of the strength that you have
because everyone suffers
but not everyone decides to heal
and healing is not for the weak.

they tell me forgiveness
is for me,
a gift I give to myself,
but everyone speaks
so highly of forgiveness,
until it is them
that have something to forgive.
I keep it in my pocket
for I am not ready
to give myself this gift.
one day, I might need it
when the healing is complete.

I think it's time
to write down lost wishes
and broken promises
and tuck them deep inside these dark clouds
that have been circling for way too long.
I can lock them inside a tiny wooden box
and throw it far out into the sea.
I think it's time to watch the sun
finally come out to play,
to hunt for mushrooms in the forest
and imagine what it's like to live in a tree.
I think it's time to buy myself flowers
to celebrate being the love of my own life.
I think it's time to heal.

I gave everyone watered down
versions of myself to drink.
I did not see the value in myself
so, I looked for it
in the reflection in their eyes.
I carefully chose how much
and how often
they'd get to take me in
it turns out,
the only validation I needed
was from myself.
once I realized
I am an acquired taste
but still a good woman
still worthy
and true love is without conditions.

"you're just too much," he said.
"I can't handle it.
go be someone else's piece of work."

I will.
I will take all those sticks and stones
with me
and use them
to no longer be your piece of work
but now my own masterpiece.

imagine.

to not be buried by
their sticks and stones
but to use them
to rebuild yourself
better than before.

know this,
you may have left me at ground zero
but I grew to be taller
than either of us could've ever imagined.

when I die,
I hope I can simply turn into colors
so, you can still find me in desert sunsets,
the ones you can't quite describe
or maybe the glitter in freshly fallen snow
before anyone has touched it.

I don't think there will come a time when I accomplish something and not quickly turn to look behind me. to search for eyes as brown as mine, to search for the ones who brew me into existence. to find some sort of approval, a nod, a gesture. words of affirmation. I don't think there will ever come a time when I don't secretly seek their love. it could almost be described as something I miss, until I realize it's impossible to miss something that I probably never had. mourning would be the more proper term for it. maybe none of us ever stop doing this. we just end up learning to swim without them because we can't drown with them anymore.

could there be anything more beautiful
than a woman's body,
especially one that tells the many stories
of the different lives she's lived?
her eyes surrounded by delicious crinkles
evidence of all the times she's laughed
her navel, now soft
that stretched to grow life.
her breasts, once sat nice and high
now hang lower but stronger,
they tell of tender times
of nourishing her young
and all the hours she spent watching them
feed until they fell asleep.
the lines between her eyes
speak of deep anger that she never let you see.
her back is tired but strong
carrying the weight of the world
and even perhaps the weight of yours.
could there be anything more magnificent
than a woman
as she can create worlds
with her bare hands.
and as one day, she will lay to finally rest,
she won't have to remind you what she's done
since her work will speak for her.

when you finally find your voice,
not everyone will like it
and some may not stay.
your voice will draw lines in the sand
and those lines will create boundaries.
those boundaries will end up protecting you
from the people
who benefitted from you having none.

never lower your voice again

you tried to walk away
and tried even harder to erase me,
burning every page in your story
that mentioned me
so no one could ever read it.

you can try to forget me
but you'll never escape my voice
and the words that immortalize your sins.

I speak for the many previous versions of me,
from the lost little girl
to the scared adolescent
to the young broken-hearted wife.
I speak for them because they had no voice
and now I am loud enough for all of us.

writers are dangerous
because poetry is easy

all you do is simply tell the truth.

it takes a brave person
to sit in their pain
and just be.

I am the result
of people not loving me
who were supposed to.
but once I understood
that it had nothing to do with me
and everything to do with their incapacity
to do so,
I broke free
and lived on.

I close my eyes
and smile softly to myself.
it's time for the show to end.
my performance wasn't pristine-
and my timing was off
but damn, did I know how
to make an impression.
this act will be tough to follow
and I pity the woman who tries
the time has come,
take a bow.

sweet girl,
I'm so sorry I had to leave you there.
I tried to pave a safe road for us,
I just never accounted
for me not knowing how.
with a kiss on your forehead,
I whispered to you
"I'll come back for you."
and now, I found you
frozen in time
in that same field of wildflowers
picking at them,
finding daisies,
bringing them to your lips,
putting them in your pocket for later
hoping to place them all around
in places you felt were needed.
with a smile, you turn to me,
"I knew you'd be back someday."
now I am running towards you.
I have stopped running away from you.
I scooped you up and took you in my arms.
I will never again let you go.

ABOUT THE AUTHOR

here I am
naked before the world
having shed layer upon layer
of all the ways I've loved others wrong
and myself not enough.
here I am
standing before you.
hello, it's nice to meet you.

my name is Jessica.
I was made to break wide open
so that others
could look through the cracks
on my body
and find the faces of all the women
that I carry with me,
the ones that fought hard to become
the woman that they are today,
the ones who never gave in
and the ones who loved
to the bitter end.
hear their voices echoing
through my words.
I was meant to bleed for them
so not one of their heartbreaks
were ever in vain.

Anna Victoria was named after my mother-in-law Victoria Ann and was born during the hardest year of my life. I did not have a voice back then, and her birth helped me find it. I now speak loudly enough for the previous versions of me who could not speak.

the birth flower of April is a daisy. Anna represents a daisy. it took finding Anna to learn how to find myself.

on the chapter title pages, the small girl represents me as a child. the adult woman is me now. I had to go back in time to rescue the girl I left behind and now together we are healing.

other titles by the author

the author's personal journey of the building,
destruction, and reconstruction of a family
affected by addiction told through poetry

let's connect
Instagram: @letters.to.anna

Made in United States
North Haven, CT
22 March 2023

34418811R00096